A Broken Cl

By: Jasmen Howard

My Bio

As a child I was raped, molested, and abused mentally and emotionally, as I moved from different foster homes, group homes, shelters, or wherever else I could lay my head.

Growing up this way made me approach life from a different aspect. Having no stability I pretty much formed my own life. I was introduced to a lot of things in this world, things that any child at any age should not be exposed to.

I dedicate this book to my children, Nikaiyah, KaiAsia, Lonnie IV, Isaiah, Jayden, Jo'el, Mia, Jayla, and if God blesses me with anymore children, than to you as well. Yes I am a Mother of 8 wonderful children.

I wrote A Broken Child as an awareness to my children, other parents, counselors, Division of Youth and Family

Services and any other sources that deal with children who grow up in and out of the system.

I want others who grew up like me and those who may go through something similar, I want them to know that there is a brighter side to life and that they no longer have to be a victim anymore.

I am open to any speaking engagements or anything that will help get awareness out to all whom will listen.

Chapter 1
Taken

At the age of 5, all I could remember was sitting in a room surrounded with a lot of people, me and my little brother Bailey. There were a lot of strange people talking to us and we had no clue who they were. They told us that they would be taking us to live with another family. At the time I didn't even remember much about my old family.

All I remember is a vision of me, a man, and a woman sitting under this house that had a lot of stairs on the outside. We were sitting at a picnic table eating a bologna and cheese sandwich. Well the two people turned out to be my biological mom and dad. Those were the only memories I had of them at the time. Anyway these two strangers told me to come to them, while they left Bailey behind.

We pulled up to a strange looking house. An elderly lady was standing on the porch. As we were getting out of the car, she walked over to greet me. "Hi, my name is Lee Bell, but you can call me grand mom from now on", she said. Before departing away from the two stranger people who brought me there, they had announced that this would be my new home for awhile.

A lot was going through my mind. I was very nervous and I was a child so I really didn't know too much about what was going on. All I knew is that I had to follow instructions and do as they told me. I also kept asking myself, "Where in the world was Baily at." It was a mystery.

Grand mom than took me in the house to show me around. She showed me the whole house including my room. There were only two rooms. Mine and grand moms. In my room there was a bunk bed, a dresser, and a cedar chest. A cedar chest looked just like a big dresser that you can store clothes and stuff in. When I saw the bunk bed I had already made in my mind that I wanted to sleep at the bottom. I didn't want to fall off in the middle of the night. Ha ha.

Down the hall from grand mom room there was something that I called the mysterious door. It was located in the weirdest spot. When grand mom opened the door there she pointed to an attic. Aside from the stairs that lead to the attic there was another door. She opened that one and there was a whole new house behind that door. I was so amazed. I had never seen anything like it before.

She began to explain to me that her great granddaughter lived on that part of the house. Her name was Julie, but of course I was to call her Aunt Julie. Grand mom was very big on respecting our elders. Aunt Julie had three children. Keisha, Sasha, and Jabree. I got alone better with Keisha because she was around my age; the other two were a couple years older than us.

Their house was so nice on the other side. I have never seen a house connected together like that... The attic really belonged to Aunt Julie. She called that the family room, where everyone could go and watch TV and play games and stuff. It was always fun up there.

I was in enrolled into school right from the start. The school was actually right down the street from the house so we walked there everyday. I started in Kindergarten and after that I ended up repeating the same grade because I was so far behind that I had to play catch up. I met so many people while going to school. I was a very sociable person.

Throughout my years of going to that school I only got in trouble twice. One incident was when I brought home a fundraiser for candy bars and tried to sell it myself. I did not tell grand mom that I had it. I tried to sell some to the neighbors on my street but no one would buy any. So as each day went on I began to eat a piece of the candy, sometimes even two pieces. I continued on everyday eating this candy until it was no more left. When it came time to hand in the money, there was no money, so the school asked for the box of candy bars back. Well apparently I didn't have them either.

When I got home that day, grand mom said she wanted to talk to me. I automatically new exactly what it was about. She says, "Where is this box of candy that the school called here about?" I lied and said that I didn't know. So she made me sit there until I decided to tell the truth. I came out and told her that I had eaten them all. Oh boy, I got my butt whipped because I told the truth; I should have just stuck with the lie, smh (shaking my head). It seemed like I spent a whole month paying for my debt because grand mom had to pay all the money back for the candy bars. One thing I know is that candy paid off for all that nasty but healthy food that she made me eat.

I had no clue to as if why I did the things that I did. Was I acting out because of my circumstances or was I just a rebellious child. Was I a drug baby? I was born at only 3 pounds. That's why I had to be rushed to a different city to be born. These are the questions that go through my mind.

Maybe one day I will get all the answers I seek and want. Who knows, only time will tell.

Chapter 2
New Experiences

One day I was at home lying on the floor coloring in my coloring book. I remember having on one of my little princess night gowns. I loved that night gown. Moments later Jabree came walking through my room door. He gets next to me and asked what I was doing. Next he says he wants to show me something. So he tells me to come lay on my bed on my stomach. I laid on my stomach. He climbs on my back and penetrates me. I kept saying it hurt and that it felt like I had to go to the bathroom. So he let me get up to go use the bathroom. I could not move my bowels. So when I got back into the room he tells me to go back on my stomach. As I lay there it still feels like have to move my bowels. I could not understand it.

I kept telling him that it hurt so he told me to lie on my back. I lay on my back. He tries to do it that way. It still hurt but it did not feel like I had to move my bowel this time. I kept squirming around and saying it hurt, so he just got up off of me and went back across to his house. I laid there for a minute crying, then I got back on the floor and finished coloring in my book as if nothing happened.

Things kept happening to me in that house. I could not understand why.

For example my cousin Sasha who was Jabree sister, was a couple years older than me. She was very aware of the things that she would do. One night we were all in the attic playing around. Sasha had this cover that she kept throwing over our heads so that everyone would be in the dark. Every time we put the cover over our heads she would reach out and touch me in a weird way. When the cover game was over we all sat down to play Nintendo.

Grand mom was pretty strict on time, so I already knew that I had to be back across the hall on time, even if it was right next door. After I went back home I sat in my room to play with my toys. Grand mom was downstairs in the living room. While I was in my room I heard the upstairs door shut. Guess who than comes walking in my room. Yes, Sasha. When she walked in she grabs my hand and pulls me off the floor. She than puts my back up against the closet door, while she stands in front of me. Sasha than lifts up my shirt and begins to rub her hands all over my chest. It than went from her hands to her mouth being all over me. Didn't know what to think or how to feel. I just knew that this was happenening. Moments later she took my hands and put them on her chest, which was much more developed than mine. As she placed my hands there she said silently, "don't be afraid, you can touch mine too." We both stood there fondling each other's chest for while. I didn't know what I was doing but I went along with it. I knew for a fact that I liked Sasha's encounter more than Jabree's. Sasha did not hurt me at all.

I was happy that Aunt Julie and them lived next door, because when grand mom had to run out and go somewhere, all she had to do was called next door and ask them to keep an eye out on me. Grand mom had to run out to the store and did not feel like lugging me with her, I guess. She turned the TV on to cartoons and told me that she would be back.

So I'm sitting down watching TV and all of a sudden, this heavy set man comes down the steps. It's obvious that he came from the inside of Aunt Julie's house. "You must be Jasmine," he said. I thought to myself, how in the world did he know my name. For now on he said he would call me bones. He introduced himself to be my Uncle James. He said "Come over and give Uncle James a hug." So I did exactly as he said.

At first the hug felt kind of weird. Than he did the obvious. As he was hugging me, he slowly backed me up against the wall. He positioned my body toward him, face to face. Then he began to feel all over my body. The weirdest part about it is that he was talking to me the whole time he did it. Asking me stupid random questions about myself. His hand began to go further and further done my little old body, until he reached my private area. His big rough hands hurt while he rubbed all over my private area. It didn't feel good at all. It felt like a rock scrapping against me.

He asked me to open my legs and I said no, repeatedly over and over again. Then he pinched and pulled my private area hard so that I would open my legs. Eventually I gave in because he did it harder and harder each time I said no. Tears rolled down my eyes as he had hurt me by squeezing so tight. He slid his finger in and out of my private area. I was scared the whole time.

The next thing he did was reach his hand in his pocket and pulled out a shinny wrapper. It was known to be a condom. Which I had no idea at the time. He unzipped his pants and put it on. Then he laid me on the floor and he put himself inside of me. It hurt just like it did with Jabree but worse. But after awhile I just pretended to be invisible and I didn't feel the pain anymore. Until this day I don't understand why I didn't scream, kick, fight, or try to get away. I sat there and let him do his deed to me. When he got done he got up and left as if he didn't do anything at all. I went upstairs and I felt something funny in my underwear. It was blood. I hurried up and took them off and hid them in the cedar chest in my room so that grand mom wouldn't find them. That didn't work out to well because one day she found them and thought I came on my menstrual cycle. She yelled at me and told me that all I had to do was say something instead of hiding my underwear. This was the first time but not the last time that Uncle James had done this to me.

Grand mom still wasn't back yet and no one still didn't come to check on me. I just laid in my bed and fell asleep, until grand mom came home.

Chapter 3
A Visitor

Things were going quite smoothly and grand mom was filled with so many surprises. However this time she said it was a special surprise. She said that my surprise wouldn't be there until later on tonight. I was so anxious to find out what it was.

Time slowly began to wind down. Next thing you know the door bell rang. Grand mom gets up to open the door. When the door opened I was so happy to see the person standing on the other side. It was my biological brother Bailey. My baby brother. Bailey came to visit and stay with us for a little while. All me, him, and Keisha did was play all day. Sometimes we got a little out of control and grand mom made us sit down and sent Keisha back next door. That particular night Baily and I ended up going to bed early; we were tired anyway from all that playing around.

The next day the social worker came and took us to go see our mom. She lived in Trenton with my biological grand mom. Our moms name was Dee. When we pulled up it was to the house I remembered that had all the steps on the outside. I had one sister named Kendal and three bothers named Jimmy, Anthony, and of course Bailey. Kendal and Anthony didn't get placed in foster care they ended up staying with my grand mom, I guess because they were the oldest. There were a lot of people who lived in that house. Including my two aunts and their kids, which were my cousins. The social worker left us there for a couple hours so we could spend time with our family.

We only ended up going there around three times because we were not supposed to be around our mom considering that she had lost all her rights to be around us until we turned eight teen years old. I didn't know back than about why we were taken but it wasn't much I can do at the time because I was a child.

Bailey stayed with us a little while longer. I had my days where I would sneak downstairs to get something to eat and Bailey would be right behind me. We both was so hungry because everything that grand mom gave us was healthy but indeed nasty. We would sneak and eat snacks like ice cream, cake, and drank some juice to wash it down. Than we both would creep back upstairs into our room.

Everything was going smoothly up until the day I got caught. Grand mom was cleaning our room and went up under the bed and found all the wrappers and stuff that we hid under the bed. I got my butt whipped for that too. Not Bailey cause grand mom said I was the one that influenced him to do it. After a while it was time for Bailey to leave. I was going to miss my little brother. It was definitely different without him there.

I wouldn't say that I was defiant or could I have been. Hmmmm, definitely something to think about. So I would stay out of some trouble grand mom got Aunt Julie to sign me up to play softball and soccer. I hated softball, not to mention that Aunt Julie was the couch for that. I did love soccer though, my favorite sport. When it came down to soccer I played the positions center and center striker. These positions were for the good players on the team, and I was very happy to be in that category. With softball, I was not good at it. Every time I played Aunt Julie yelled at me.

One day I was up to bat and she kept yelling, "hit the ball Jasmine." I got so angry at her yelling at me that I took it out on the ball. I had missed the first two hits before she started yelling at me. But that third time I balled up all my anger that I had for her and I hit that ball so hard that it flew right at the pitcher and struck her right in the stomach. She fell to the ground and as she cried and held her stomach. She ended up being removed from the game so that she could recover. Aunt Julie was so proud of me hitting that ball that I don't even think she first realized the pitcher was hurt. Oh and for the record, just because I hit the ball doesn't mean that I like softball anymore than I did before I hit it, lol.

Every time something happen with me, grand mom told Aunt Amy. Aunt Amy was Uncle James sister and Aunt Julie's sister as well. Aunt Amy always told grand mom that she was too old to be taking care of me. But Gran mom never listened to her.

Until one late afternoon, it was pouring down raining. Grand mom had told me to go and get ready because my social worker was coming to take me to see my mom. I was confused though because my mom lost all her rights and they said that was our last time going there.

Earlier that day before this happened. I told Keisha to tell Jimmy that I like him. Jimmy was a boy that lives next door to us. He was light-skinned it and very cute. I was supposed to meet him outside that night but grandma would not let me go out in the rain. So when I came outside to leave with my worker, I saw Keisha and Jimmy down the street standing under the umbrella staring at me. I feel so embarrassed because I did not have time to react. At this point I knew that Keisha had told Jimmy already that I like him. As I got in the car I said to myself I'll just wait next time when I see him to react, not knowing that there would be no next time. All my worker kept saying was that we were going for a ride. The more we rode around the more I began to notice that we were not going to see my mom.

You will never guess where we ended up at. Yes, we were at Aunt Amy's house. I knew I would feel comfortable at Aunt Amy house only because she had four adoptive kids living with her already. There were three boys, all younger than me, and a girl name Rasha who was older than all of us.

As we waited for her to come out the house my worker told me that this would be my new house. I was kind of happy for two reasons. One, I did not have to eat that nasty food anymore and I did not have to wear those clothes anymore. I remember every day taking my purple dress to school and I would change in the bathroom and wear that dress almost everyday. People would stare at me because they question why I would have such a classy dress on in school. Most of the time I would lie and say that I was going to a wedding. I wore it over and over and over again and did not care about what people thought. With that dress on I felt cute I felt alive.

I found out that Grandma had had no idea that on Aunt Amy had taken me away from her. When Grandma found out she was so mad at Aunt Amy for betraying her. It took a long time for her to speak to Aunt Amy again. I was so happy to be where I was at that moment.

Chapter 5
The Move

It was around the year of 1991 and everything has changed for me. My life felt so normal staying with Aunt Amy. I had my own room and everything. But it was not going to last long because we were going to move next week.

Grand mom used to let Aunt Julie braid my hair so my hair was very long. However Aunt Amy had different plans for my hair, she ended up giving me a relaxer. She knew how to do hair very well. When she got done putting my relaxer in, she clipped my ends as well. My hair looked like a mushroom. It was nice and bouncy and shaky I loved it so much.

Aunt Amy was a nice person; however she was very strict as well. Every single child in the house had a chore to do. We would keep the same chores for about a week and than rotate. The biggest mistake you could ever do was fall asleep without completing your chore. You better believe Aunt Amy was waking you up out of your sleep to do that chore. With a belt at that. A lot of times she did not need a belt. She had those big black rough hands that hurt as well. Lol. Was not funny at the time though. I remember the worst punishment I ever got. It is something that I will never forget. The stairs leading from the downstairs to the upstairs had about 15 individual steps to it. When we had really done something out of the ordinary, Aunt Amy made us run up and down the steps about fifty times. The worst part is that if we fell we had to start all over again. I fell a whole lot of times. Sometimes she would have mercy on us and let us stop. She was too strict for me. We were not allowed to talk back to our elders, no sucking our teeth, no nothing. I almost regret leaving grand mom house. It's funny because my kids get away with more than they should because some of them went through the sucking teeth phase. They are fortunate that I don't spank them for everything; however they will respect me and their elders.

On moving day, I really didn't have anything to pack because I had left my things at grand mom house. The things that I did have are what Aunt Amy brought me from scratch, so basically I just helped everyone else pack. We ended up moving to the other side of town. The section that people called Westside.

The day that we moved in we had a lot of things that we had to do to fix the house up. It was a nice big house too. I mean huge. Three families could fit in that one house. Most of the work had to be done on the third floor. We had to tear down parts of the ceiling, so that they could put new ones in. It was kind of easy. All we had to do was push the ceiling boards up with the broom and they popped right out.

There were these square brown pieces of sponge things under the boards. I will never ever touch those things ever again. These brown things made us itch so bad that we thought we had to go to the hospital and get a shot or something. We itched and itched and itched. We scratched and scratched and scratched. It actually felt like bugs was crawling on us. End result, Aunt Amy told all of us to go take a shower. She fiddled around in our bags trying to find all of our soap and rags and everything that we needed at the moment.

There were two showers so she split the boys up into one bathroom and the girls into another one. Everyone got in the shower and when we got out we were still itching. It took hours for that itch to stop. It was the worst itch of my life.

After we were done with all of the walls we all sat down to unpack our bags. Rasha and I had the rooms on the third floor. I loved it up there. It was like a little an apartment up there. The big open space we called the family room. It had a bathroom and a mini kitchen up there. The family room is where we all got together and watched TV and played games. Mostly anything we did as a family was done in the family room.

We really didn't know anyone around the area yet, however there was a park around the corner from us. It was like two parks in one that's how huge it was. One side had swings and cookout. The other had basketball court where men dressed in uniforms and battled each other every summer in basketball. They had everything out there. Hot dog stands, and the ice cream trucks were my favorite.

During the summer still seemed like being in school, because Aunt Amy worked us a lot. She was a schoolteacher, so, she kept materials for us, all the time. Usually, before we were able to go outside, we had to complete a worksheet assignment. Sometimes she would actually make it fun and interesting. She would divide us up into teams and we would have Math Jeopardy or History Trivia. It was so much fun.

She was mean as she could be, but she eased up on us once she got her boyfriend Breon. He was Haitian and made some good Haitian food too. She became a little a Haitian woman herself. She started talking like him and all. At the time he was ok in my book, until one night, I was laying in my bed asleep. I was never the type who sleeps hard. I could hear a needle drop when I'm sleep. I heard my door creak open. I pretended I was sleep. He came over to my bed, leaned over me and put his hand down my shirt. Then I turned over to pretend as if I was still sleep. He began to rub all over my chest. Then he saw that I had no reaction. So he slowly shook me, trying to wake me up.

I turned over now and said, "What do you want?" He then, put his tongue in my mouth trying to kiss me! I pushed him away.

He said, "Come on baby, I want you to be my girlfriend." I looked at him like he was crazy. He kept trying to sleep with me but I keep saying no. But that didn't stop him from continuously sneaking in my room touching me and he would do it any time of the day, whether it was morning noon or night. As long as he didn't see anyone around. Even when he did hear people coming he would just hurry and move away from me. At one point in time, Aunt Amy had sat down and asked me and Rasha what we thought about Breon. Rasha said that she thought he was ok. I said that I thought that he was too friendly. She didn't know what I meant when I said too friendly but I knew. I don't know why she wanted our approvals anyway.

Chapter 6
A Special Day

Besides what happened to me with Breon, Jubree, Uncle James and Sasha, I just went on being little old me.

As a child, things like that really didn't have an effect on me. It actually affected me more as an adult. All I know is as a child when I always got in trouble and yelled at, I thought the whole world was against me. When I got angry or frustrated I would always write a poem for how I felt. Writing was one way to ease my mind. This one poem, in particular, reminds me of the way I really felt about my life. It's called A Shadow of Darkness:

As I walk steadily with a slow pace,

I could see up against the wall, a shadow
Of my face.

The streets are dark, and the winds are
Echoing through the nights. I turn in
Fear, but my shadow is all I saw. A shadow
Of fright. The crying, the mourning in
Darkness and in light. A trace of emptiness
For no one was in sight.

When you think of A Shadow of Darkness you
Think of evil, lies, hurt, suffering and sometimes
Even pain. Life is complicated and is almost never
The same.

The things covered by shadows of darkness,
things
That takes time to heal. When will this Shadow
separate
From dark to light. When will it be revealed?

When I see this shadow it represents the loneliness
of an
Empty heart. What heart is this beneath? Whose
shadow is
This that dares to come forth? Dares to sit there
and stare.
It is my shadow of darkness, my shadow of
shame, My
Shadow is unaware –

As you can see writing was my way out. Out of hurt, pain and whatever it is that I was feeling at the time. It didn't last for long though because there was a lot of fun in store for me.

Coming up was the family annual family reunion. That is where our whole family drove to another state to reunite with other family members from all over. Than after the reunion we always went to another state for vacation, like Florida. Fun, fun, fun. I loved Universal Studios the most.

Our reunions really didn't consist of that much. We rented trailer, which I hated because of those loud crickets chirping all night. We went out on paddle boats, and they were so much fun too. But most of all, my ultimate favorite was karaoke night. I just like to sing my little heart out. I always loved to sing, even though I wasn't that great at it. So the second day was the actual reunion. Boring, boring, and boring. I didn't know any of those people anyway.

Vacation time was always the best for me like I mentioned, however that all changed one day. Now, I was always scared of roller coasters. One day I, Aunt Amy and the other kids were waiting to go on the batman ride. I got all the way to the top and changed my mind about getting on. So Aunt Amy told me to sit in the chair and it will take me back around so that I could get off because it was too many people in line to turn around and go back down. And of course I listened to her and sat down. The next thing you know. Those bars closed down on me and than the coaster began to move. I started screaming and crying really loud. I cried from the time I sat down until the time I got off the ride. I was so mad at Aunt Amy; I thought I would never get over it. Eventually I did, but I can tell you that I never got on another roller coaster again.

After vacation, it usually took about two and a half days to get back home. The ride was fun for us kids because all we had to do was sleep the whole way. I kind of got along with all my siblings. I guess it's because we all were foster kids, so we felt no different.

Around 1989, Aunt Amy made a decision that was going to change all of our lives. That day she told all of us to get in the car and that we were going somewhere special. We were all excited and could not wait. We pulled up in front of a courthouse. She pulled me to the side and told me that we were here so that she could adopt me. That meant that legally I would be her daughter. As we sat down with the judge she said that my middle and last name could get changed. So I walked in the courtroom as Jasmine Nicole Tift and I walked out as Jasmen Amy Howard. They had made an error on the spelling of my first name. However as an adult I can fix it. As a child, the error was permanent on my new birth certificate.

Anyway, I was now a Howard, but the person in side of me remains the same. I guess what mattered more is that I didn't have to worry about going to another foster home that made me happy.

Chapter 7
New School Environment

It was almost time for the school year to begin. Things were still the same. Breon was still touching on me every now then. Uncle James was still having sex with me. One time Uncle James came over to the house and told Aunt Amy that he needed me to come help him clear out some stuff in his attic. And she freely let me go with him. I knew what he was going to do every time he asked if I could go with him. He always called me bones because I was so skinny as a child.

Back then I didn't know that it was called rape and molestation. When he took me to his house over the bridge. No one knew we were there but Aunt Amy. He would lay me on the floor and do his thing. And afterwards he would always give me a couple of dollars. Now that I'm grown and understand it more, I think he was giving me the money so that I could be happy and not run back and tell anyone.

There were even times where he had pool parties or cookouts at his house. When there were cookouts and he saw me go into the house to use the bathroom, he would follow me in there, pin me against the wall, and rub his hand all around my private area. He didn't care that he had a backyard full of family, he did it anyway. However, he didn't do it for long because he knew eventually someone might come in the house and catch him. At the pool parties it was different. When we all were in the pool, he would play this game where he would go under the water and put our legs around his neck and push us out of the water. Every time he did that to me, he reached his hands under my bathing suit to feel my private area.

All the times that he had sex with me, I just lay there with no sound, no emotion, or reaction. It was as if I was dead, but alive. He didn't care where he had sex with me at. It was mostly at his house when his wife wasn't there, and mostly in his jeep. He usually pulls into an empty parking lot and does it in his jeep. And one time in his family trailer. He was convinced that he could have me whenever he wanted. I was his mate.

Anyhow, I was looking forward to starting school. Aunt Amy wasn't too fond of us going to public school so she sent all of us too a Christian School. We had to wear uniforms and everything. I started there in the fifth grade. I was already behind a grade from when I stayed back in kindergarten from starting school late. It really wasn't too much to the fifth grade. I met a lot of new people there. However, I only considered one person to be a close friend of mine and her name was Rosaline. She was Spanish, with long pretty black hair, and she was so short, lol. (Laughing out loud) She was absent a lot because she was always sick, so the days she wasn't there I really missed her.

Then we had this girl in our class who was a little off and she always passed gas and picks her nose all the time.

I can remember my first crush. It was with a boy named, Rob. He was white as the snow and I was brown skinned, I didn't care because he was perfect to me. He knew that I liked him. I followed him everywhere. I even tried to sit by him all the time. Every year we had Carnation Day. On Carnation Day everyone would order carnation flowers of various colors and give them to whomever they wanted. White and pink stood for friendship and red stood for love. Of course you should know what color I sent to Robby. Yes, red of course. However, I don't think he felt the same way about me because I never got one from him. It didn't matter that I didn't get one from him. It had no affect on me.

My crush for Robby didn't last long. I had forgotten about him especially when they sent me to my right grade. In the 6th grade I met a girl named Carmen. No one really liked her because she thought she was all that. She was very sloppy though. This girl is so loud and wild. She danced around a lot, and was so hyperactive. Her being hyperactive made her have a lot of accidents while she was on her menstrual cycle. A couple of times she would get up out of her seat and have accidents all on her pants that never fazed her though. She still danced and did everything. I hated being on my menstrual so I stayed as still as possible. Lol (laughing out loud).

My school was kind of interesting. The will have what u call field days. They were inside of the school. They had so many different booths with games. My favorite one was the fish booth. We could actually play a game and win a fish. Every time I took my fish home they died.

I tried to do some things to stand out in school. I loved to sing so I tried out for the choir. A couple of my friends tried out and we made it. Rosaline and Robby made it too.

I loved that school so much. They really had a lot to offer. I missed my old class but I still do every now and then. Also Rosaline had sleep over's at her house all the time so, I was good.

One day that all changed because Aunt Amy decided to take us out of our school. She decided to put us in the Neighborhood School which was just down the street. It was so easy to get to that school. The only fear I had was starting all over again and making new friends on over again. One thing I noticed is that I did not like change this was one thing that still stuck with me throughout my life today.

Chapter 8
Betrayed

When I started Public School down the street from the house, I saw there a lot of people that I went to elementary school with so I was really familiar with a lot of people. The more and more I went to school the more I realize that I do not like school. Every morning I got up and I went to school a little early just so that I and the girls can play double dutch every morning. I was really good at Double Dutch as a child I was really good at a lot of things, you name it I was good at it.

One day I went to school and guess who I ran into, Carmen the girl that went to a Christian school with me. She and I became real good friends and her mom even came to pick me up from Amy house to take me to their Church from time to time. Actually I was going quite often to church and it became my home Church. Her mom was a very spiritual person and she had a good heart as well.

I remember one day I went to school I was very upset because the night before Breon had snuck into my room again. I was really getting tired of it; it was a lot to cope with even more than what Uncle James was doing to me. The reason why I felt this way it's because Breon live with us so it was hard because he can come into my room every night if he wanted to. When Uncle James violated me it was not every day because he did not live there. So I already was mad that morning and have an attitude in school and was feeling kind of down and one of my friends asked me what was wrong with me, so I told her what Breon was doing to me. I was so mad at her because I told her that as a friend and she turned around and told one of our teachers and our teacher confronted me and asked me if it was true. I told her yes it is true, so she said that she will have to contact my parent to notify her about what was told to her.

After school my teacher ended up coming to our house and she sat down to talk to Aunt Amy and told Aunt Amy what I had told her. After they got finished talking my teacher left. Later on that night around 1 a.m. in the morning the cops came knocking at the door. Apparently my teacher has reported the incident and the cops began to ask me questions about what happened. I told them everything that happened in all the stuff that Breon was doing to me and they call Breon in the room to question him and ask him did he ever do anything to violate me and of course he denied it. So after the police had left Aunt Amy said that she did not believe me and neither did the police because my story was not consistent. I said to myself how can they not believe me, because first of all I was a child second of all I don't record everything that he does to me on what days all I know is that he creeps into my room and he touches me, so what if I didn't have all of the dates that they wanted me to have down pack the facts were, that he was touching me that's all they needed to know.

So being that they did not believe me nothing was done he still continue to live in the house and she still continues to be with him. He still continued to touch me and he still continues to get away with it. I feel very betrayed my Aunt Amy for still allowing him to live there after knowing what he could have done to me but hey she did not believe me so why not keep him as her man.

As the years begin to fly by I begin to get really rebellious. I had so much anger toward her that I did not listen to nothing that she told me to do. Being that I was a child people could take advantage of me. Why on Earth would I even attempt to tell her anything else when she did not even believe what I told her about her man?

I can't even begin to express how I feel about Aunt Amy right now. I wonder if I was her biological daughter would she have believed me?

There was no way possible that Uncle James would ever get caught now because it's obvious that she would have not believed me about him either.

Our school was offering pre-college programs and I filled out an application. The program would be held during the summer time at the college. It was a program where we had to be accepted. When I got my acceptance letter in the mail I was so happy, I was so excited. The program consists of us going for the summer each year until we graduated so I was looking forward to spending the summer there with my friends because they also got accepted. The crazy part is one day I remember Aunt Amy saying to me did I want to go to the program so that I can get away for awhile because evidently she noticed how upset I was after the incident with the cops and Breon. So I told her yes I want to go to the program since I was accepted it anyway.

Chapter 9
True Colors

One day I ended up falling asleep without doing my dishes. So Aunt Amy came and woke me up so that I can do my dishes, the whole time I'm doing my dishes I'm mad and crying with an attitude. Aunt Amy and I ended up exchanging words and next thing you know she said if you don't like it then you can get out of my house. At the time I was 14 years old. So my response to her was okay I'm leaving so I threw the dish rag down and walked out the door. Back then in a lot of areas they had payphones.

So I ended up roaming around neighborhood trying to find somewhere to go. I ended up talking to one of my cousins who told me where my biological mom lives at so I went to her house and I found her and she let me stay with her for a couple of months. I did not feel comfortable there because she was on drugs but at the time I had nowhere else to go.

After being there for a while I got in contact with Amy and I told her where I was. She asked me if I still wanted to go to the college program and I said yes so she brought me a whole bunch of stuff to get ready to go to the college program. Being that I had run away from home I missed my 8th grade graduation. I had a couple of months to go before I went to the college program so I just stayed at my biological mom house for those couple of months. Uncle James found out where I live. So he started coming around there more often. He had like this purplish Jeep that no one could miss. I should not have been surprised being that he was Amy's brother that eventually he would know where I was. So he came by and told me to get in his car and take me somewhere to do his business like usual and each time he still handed me money. I would get so mad because every time he gave me money I had put it up inside the house and my biological mom would steal it to go buy her drugs. I was so upset every time this happened I said to myself that I had to hurry up and find somewhere else to sleep.

While I was there I met this guy who was 27 years old I ended up being in a relationship with him his name was Charles. Yes as you can see I was only 14 and he was 27 however I was a child and I knew nothing about age limits or anything. Being with him I was introduced to a lot of things I started smoking weed I started drinking and I was independent so basically I did what I want I had no authority or anything. One day he took me to one of his friends house and while I was there I saw two females who were lesbians and I was walking into one of the rooms and I saw them too being intimate with each other I hurried up and I turned around and walked away. As I was sitting on the bed in another room one of the girls came into the room and ask me if she could be intimate with me. I had no idea of what it would be like because I had never made a choice to be with someone like that however this was not like the incident where Sasha touched all over me at Grandma's house. I came right out and told her yes, you can be intimate with me.

At that moment she had took me to a whole different level my very first full sexual encounter with a female. It was so weird to me because I actually liked it. This girl I had never been intimate with her again instead I begin to see her friend that was in the room with her. We had became really close and ended up being in a very close relationship. She was named after a calendar month. Her name was July. There was something very special about July. We hung out we did everything together I ended up leaving my biological mom's house and sometimes I would stay the night at July's house her parents didn't care she was actually 13 one year younger than me and she ran the streets and did whatever she wanted to do as well. I was so in love with this girl, we were together morning noon and night everyday all day.

Until one day my worker found me and ended up taking me to stay in the shelter at the anchor house. I stayed there and I still had to go to school and stuff. I would walk from the shelter all the way to school. That was my first year of high school. I hated school with a passion. All I could think about was July, but I was not worried because I knew that eventually I will meet up with her again. I barely made it through my 9th grade year even though I was at the shelter it didn't stop me from still running the streets, they threatened to kick me out a couple times. But I didn't care anyway, all I know is that I was considered a runaway and I was free and no one could tell me what to do.

I was so happy that I made it through that first year of high school. Aunt Amy came and picked me up to take me to the college program. When I got there I was so amazed. I was so happy to see all my friends again and to actually be in that type of setting. The campus was so huge. We live in one of the dormitories and we shared a room with one other person. Of course we could not request who we room with they just placed us with anybody. During the day we would take different types of pre college classes that prepare us for college and in between classes we will have free time to do whatever we please to do. The place where we ate at was in a different building and it was called, The Commons. When I say Buffet heaven it was like a buffet for breakfast lunch and dinner we could go up and get as many portions as we choose. I really like going there, but throughout the whole thing all I could think of was July. Because it seems like throughout all that I have been through she was the only one that knew and understood me.

While I was there I ended up having a conversation with one of my teachers her name was Sherry. I kind of told Sherry my story and how I did not have a place to stay. So at the end of the program Sherry took me to her house to meet her mom. They ended up letting me spend the night there and the next day Sherry had a talk with her mom and her mom said that I could stay there for a while. So she got in contact with my worker and they gave her temporary custody of me. All together her mom had 5 children. She also had another man that she called her son but he was not really her son. At first I liked it there, but then I begin to notice that she treated me differently from her own children. She will make me get up every morning early to walk her daughter to the bus stop. I just knew that it felt different from any other place that I was at.

Chapter 10
Different

So, I decided to do what I wanted to do and be rebellious. I had a boyfriend and sometimes instead of going to school I will go to his house. After a while she started to see my rebellious ways and knew that she could not handle me so she turned me back over to my worker. My worker took me back to the Anchor house once again. That didn't keep me inside. I still ran the streets. I still went to see my boyfriend, and I still was seeing July as well. I did not really like boys too much so I stopped seeing my boyfriend and I continue to see July. I felt so free with July; we were both free when we were together, and free to do anything that we wanted to do.

I was happy anyway not to be at Sherry's mom's house anymore because her son liked me and I can remember on two occasions him sticking his fingers in my pants. And also her son that she called her son which really wasn't her son took me to his house one day and tried to have sex with me. I kept telling him no he tried to pull down my pants and I held my pants tight so that he could not succeed and pulling them down. Finally he gave up and took me back to Sherry mom house. One thing I will never understand is why people always had to do sexual things to me; I will never understand how I always went through this. I always wonder if it was my fault that all these things are happening to me?

Being back at the shelter was no surprise to me it was almost like my second home. Every time I come there sometimes I would see the same faces of other kids and sometimes I will see new faces. But every time the staff member saw me back there they gave me this hopeless look. After awhile I could not take it being at the shelter anymore so I ran away from there once again. This time I went to my biological cousin's house. Both of my aunts had a house together. I hang closer to my cousin Kia. At times I hated going there to stay for a couple nights. I can still here my aunt's voice saying "those worker people better not come knocking on my door looking for you." So I made my days there very limited because I did not want to hear her mouth about that.

It all was becoming a little overwhelming for me; I was getting tired of trying to find a place to stay every night. The only reason why I kept a couple of dollars in my pocket is because every time Uncle James picked me up to do his thing with me, he gave me money. This went on for so many years that I felt like he owned me. As an adult, I realize that growing up as a child, I was considered his trick. This is the name they give women who have sex for money. I get a nasty feeling every time I think of it. How can a man take advantage of a child for all those years?

Anyway, I wandered around the city for days like usual. It was a matter of time before I was caught by my worker again. Every time he found me he would give me a little pep talk. I think he cared about me just a tad bit. He ended up taking me back to the shelter again. This time when I went back, the staff said that they think I need something more permanent to stay. They had me fill out this questionnaire; it had all types of questions on it. They asked me if I smoked weed or if I drank so I said yes. So they came up with the idea to send me to Secaucus New Jersey to a program. I went there and once again it was other teenagers like me. I hated that place with a passion. I could not roam around there like I could at the shelter, they had us on lockdown.

That type of program had crazy intervention sessions. They would put us all in a circle and one staff would pretend to be one of the people whom we wanted to confront, whether it is someone who hurt us or violated us. When it was time for me to go, I sat there and stared at them like they was crazy. I was not trying to talk anyone about what goes on in my life. I always held my entire emotions in. after trying to reach me throughout each intervention; they finally gave up on me. I heard one of the staff members say, "There is no hope for her, she is the walking dead." Believe it or not that stuck with me for the rest of my life.

I always felt so alone as a child. There were times that they had visitor's day for family and friends to come see us and also some people got letters sent to them from their families. I had no one, so no one ever came to see me ever.

I had an attachment and abandonment issues. Everywhere I went I looked for that mother or father figure. There was a lady at the program name Ms. Lynn. I gravitated toward her. She was like a mother to me. She even said that she would adopt me if she could, but of course she couldn't. I got so attached to her and then one day they took her away from me. They ended up terminating her. After that happened I just didn't care even more about being there. My heart was broken so bad. I did not want to be there anymore.

One day a couple of us girls were talking about running away from the program. We sat down and planned the whole thing out. The plan was to wait until lunch time to run. Only because that is the only time that we had access to being outside of the building. We ate lunch in a different building. When it was lunch time we stood at the end of the line. There was never any staff at the end of the line; they stayed in the front to direct the front of the line. Soon as the staff entered the lunch room door, that was our key to run.

We darted out of that line so quickly. We ran all the way to the back of the building. In order to get off the premises we had to climb this gate that looked twenty feet tall. I did not think that I would make it over it but I did. Once we got over the gate, we ran and ran and ran so fast. The thing about the area we were in is that the streets were very long. We walked for about 20 minutes down that long street and when we turned around we saw a cop car pulling up behind us. They escorted us back to the program. The other girls got kicked out immediately. See some people were there through the court system. Actually most of them were there through the court system. I had to wait a couple of days for my worker to come pick me up. One thing the program did not tolerate is people running away. That's was immediate grounds for termination. I didn't care anyway because I hated it there.

My worker came and took me right back to my favorite spot, the Anchor House. They were not happy to see me back at all. I was tired of going there to, but at least I was back in jersey and I could go see July, my favorite girl.

Chapter 11
The last Stop

From reading my previous chapters you can see that all of this was basically routine for me. Meaning, that I went back to my regular routine. Running the streets, not going to school. They had kicked me out of the high school. I ended up going to the daylight twilight program. I went to school at night. I did not stay there though because I would not stand still. I was always roaming around. I even went back to Aunt Amy house for a couple days. I brought July over there one night. We sat on the porch, drank and smoked a little bit of weed. Plus I would leave to go spend the day with July and sometimes I wouldn't come back to Aunt Amy house until about 3 in the morning. One day when I came back late, I had a rude awakening. Aunt Amy had my small bag packed and out on the porch waiting for me. She had kicked me out. I hated her for that because it was her fault that I ran off anyway. If she would have kicked her perverted boyfriend out than I would have still been there.

I ended up catching the bus back to July house and staying there for the night. The next time I had ran out of options of who to ask if I could spend the night so I took myself back to the shelter. They got in contact with my worker to let him know that I showed up there. The next day he came and got me. He took me to a group home in Flemington New Jersey. This was more long term and since I only had about seven more months until I was eighteen this would have been my last placement.

Like any other program I have to share room with someone. I met a lot of different people there. Girls and boys lived at the group home. The boy's rooms were way on the other side of the building. I remember braiding all the Hispanic and Caucasian girls' hair. They always use to say that they wanted to try out braids because they had never had them done before. So I was the hair dresser there. Out of all the places I think this was the one I liked mostly. The director was vey mean. We called her judge Judy because she looked like her and was mean like her. I went to school out there but I always cut school. So I was never there. I began working at a supermarket out there, but I had to turn in all my money to staff so they could manage it.

I gravitated to a girl name Sandra. Sandra work at a bar. She had been in the group home for a couple of years. I actually I felt kind of bad for her. One day she said she would sneak us in some drinks. She came home with drinks in a bottle. She snuck it into her room and we all came in there and got blasted. She also gave us some cold pills to take with the drinks. I had never done anything like that before. We would have gotten away with it if it wasn't for one of the girls. This girl was so wasted; she went outside the room near the staff office staggering and all. They noticed it and questioned her and of course she spilled the beans on us all. We got in trouble but Sandra got in trouble more because she brought it into the group home. That was the last time we did anything like that. Throughout my time there I saw a lot of people come and go. I felt sorry for the people who had lived there for years. I never knew that it could be so many people in a similar situation like me.

I stayed there for my six month time period. I could not run away there, I was too far from Jersey so I sucked it up and completed my time there. A little while after my eighteen birthday my worker came and took me back to jersey. He placed me in an independent living program with some lady name Jita. Jita had three other foster girls living with her. I got along with all three of them. We were all around the same age. Two of the girls were sisters and they worked at the chicken restaurant. We use to always go there and get chicken meals for dinner. The other girl I believe I knew her from the shelter. Jita had enrolled me into the high school in the neighborhood. I was in the eleventh grade. Yeah I went through the ropes again of a new school, and meeting new friends and all. But I did not stay in one place for too long. Being that I was so rebellious , me and Jita got into it a lot, I always was a person to speak my mind, it might have always come out the wrong way but , I did speak my mind. I ended up leaving Jitas' house; I could not take it anymore. I ended up going to stay with my cousin Kia for a couple days. Now I didn't have to hear my aunt saying that she didn't want those worker people knocking on the door anymore. I was so happy that I was not in the system anymore.

While staying with my cousin I met this guy name Kane. I was not in love with Kane but we were very intimate a lot. When I say a lot I do mean a lot. We hung out just about every day. Then one day I noticed that I had missed my menstrual cycle. Took a pregnancy test and found out that I was pregnant. I told Kane about it, he denied the baby being his at first because I did sleep with this one guy, but that was months before Kane and I spent all of our time together. I did not get pregnant by Kane until months later. I found out that Kane had at least 8 other children by other women, whom I met later on and he denied those kids too. I didn't know what do think about being pregnant, but I did know that I was going to have the baby.

I stop seeing Kane after he denied getting me pregnant. I had no time for no one's crap. After staying with my cousin for a couple days, I went to stay with my other cousin name Tika. Tika and I were first cousins. Tika lived there with her brother, his wife and my aunt. They let me stay there for a couple days knowing that I was pregnant and all. Tika's brother's wife had a sister name Rhonda. Rhonda lived in an apartment and needed someone to move in to help split the bills. So I ended up moving with Rhonda. I was so happy that I had my first stable place to lay my head. I had no clue that Rhonda was interesting in girls. We had a conversation one day about females being with females and next thing you know me and her hooked up.

Ronda was married, however her husband was incarcerated. Her husband had a male friend name Kaoss. Kaoss lived in Newark. They introduced me to him and we hit it off ok. I started dating him, nothing to serious though. I never had any feelings for anyone whom had come across my life so far, accept for July. July was special to me. I ran into her after all those years and she said to me" you know you still my baby, right" I smiled with a blush and said yes.

Chapter 12
Lessons

It was around my due date time. I was a little nervous, who wouldn't be. I was going to be a first time mom, never experience the pain that everyone was preparing me for.

I remember laying on the couch and feeling thing small pains every once in awhile. Rhonda called her sister who knew a lot about having babies. Her sister told me to drink some water and lie back down because it was probably what they call Braxton Hicks contractions. Braxton hicks were false alarm contractions and a lot of women experience them at the end of their pregnancies. Rhonda was finishing up dinner. She was making shrimps with pasta. I could not wait to sink my teeth into that food, the baby was hungry too. I stood up off the couch to go in the kitchen to eat, next think you know a puddle of water runs down my legs. My water had broken. They rushed me to the hospital and eight hours later I had my oldest daughter Nikaiyah. She was born in November, fourteen days after my birthday.

She was so small and bright skinned. I held her tight and kissed on her little cheeks. I was in love at the very moment. I had someone who loved me back. We stayed in the hospital for about three days, than we went home. Kane had only seen her twice after she was born, than he went missing in action. Kaoss was basically there throughout Nikaiyah's infant days. Being a mom was not easy but I wouldn't have traded her for anything. I was on County assistance so I received help with my portion of the rent. The rest of the bills we split. The county had even given us a furniture voucher. During that time I was in touch with my biological sister Kendal. Kendal had three children but her youngest girl was only a baby. She had needed a place to stay because her and her boyfriend was having issues; I let her come stay with us. She was my only sister from my biological mom. So that made her my oldest and only sister.

About six months later after I had my oldest, I noticed that I missed another menstrual. I kept saying to myself there is no way that I could be pregnant. Took a pregnancy test and yes indeed it was positive. I let Kaoss know as soon as possible. He was so happy. Even happier when I found out she was a girl. While I was pregnant Kaoss got incarcerated. That was all I needed to deal with. I ended up getting the cable and phone bill in my name. Being that her husband and Kaoss were locked up we were accepting so many jail calls from them, it ended up running the bill sky high. I am still being haunting for that bill after all these years. They even sued me and snatched money out of my bank account. Oh yeah, they don't play.

Long story short, the bills were getting way out of hand and we ended up losing the apartment. We all had to leave. Me, Rhonda and Kendal.

I was very of upset because here I am with one child and pregnant with the next with nowhere to go. It was easy to find places for myself as a teenager but who will accept a grown woman with one child and pregnant again?

I thank God that I still kept in touch with Rasha. She opened up her home to me and my daughter. I moved into her basement. It was not a regular room but it was very spacious down there. Kaoss came to visit me from time to time.

One time he came over and he was drunk. We had a disagreement on something and he went off physically on me. He choked me up and everything. I broke away and kicked him out. I immediately ended whatever we had. I knew at that point that I did not want that in my life. I knew that if he put his hands on me that time, that he would end up doing it again. Something's I caught onto fast and some things I did not.

Receiving money from the government was nothing compared to if I had a regular nine to five job. It was really just a waste of time. That's why I needed a job as soon as possible.

Nikaiyah was going on one year old. I had a big party for her and all my family showed up. Even my biological dad that I didn't really know. I had a sister on my dad side name Tammie. Tammie and I was the same age, just born a couple days apart. I actually did not meet her until I was about fifteen. We hung out a couple times together. Even cut school together. I remember one time we cut school and started walking on the same street that she lived on. What the hell were we thinking? We got caught by her mom. She said if you two are going to cut than why cut on the same street. That was pretty stupid of us.

My sister Tammy had two other sisters who lived with her. They use to throw house parties and everything. We had so much fun during the time I was a runaway. I wish that I had grown up with all my siblings as a child.

Anyhow, the party was successful. I had a ball. After cleaning up all the mess. I took a hot bath and went to bed. I was so exhausted.

A couple of months went by and I had my second daughter KaiAsia in 2003. Now I had a one year old and a newborn. Kaoss and I were not on speaking terms but I did allow him to come to the hospital to see her.

Chapter 13
Sacrifices

Every once in awhile Aunt Amy still came by to put her little two cents in me and Rasha business. Boy did I really despise her after the situation that happened with me and Breon. I really never wanted to see her face; I just tolerated her every time I saw her. Which really wasn't much anyway because my time at Rasha house was up. It's kind of was a similar story to when me and Ronda stayed together. It was time for us to move.

I went my separate way. I ended up staying with my biological sister Kendal for a couple of months. Kendal and my biological mom lived together. While I was there, I began going to my home church that Carmen introduced me to, more often. I wanted my babies to grow up in the church as well. The more I went there, the more I loved going.

While I was going to the church, I talked to my Pastor about a lot of my struggles. He ended up signing me up for a female mentor name, May. I wonder why I keep ended up with girlfriends who have names like the calendar months. May was assigned to me because she had some of the same struggles in the past that she was delivered from. First everything started out great. Than next thing you know when we get into the topic about homosexuality it must have struck up a memory for her. Next thing you know she told me one day that I had very seductive eyes and it was over from there.

May and I had began seeing each other intimately. May was a lot larger and taller than me. She was looked like a tom boy and rough on the outside; however on the inside she was as sweet as a pie. I looked at her like she was my big cuddly bear. My daughters and I went to visit May on numerous occasions at her house. She was always welcoming to us. After being with someone and spending a lot of time with them you develop feelings for them. You don't see male nor female, you just see the inside of a person.

I had realized at that very moment that this had become one of my struggles. The fact that I loved to be with women. The reason why I say it's a struggle is because at that point in my life I was serving God and I wanted to be obedient to his word. Yes I was a baby in Christ, but at that moment I had knew that it was a sin.

One day I ran into a friend of mine and they told me about this program that offered free parenting classes. I signed up for the classes, I was always eager to learn new things. Each person was assigned a worker that checked on us monthly. I explained my living situation to my worker. She told me about this shelter that took moms and children. At this shelter they offered help with finding a place. I thought about it for a moment and I said to myself if this is the sacrifice I will have to make for my children than so be it.

I ended up moving into the shelter with my daughters. We had a room to ourselves. They provided our meals to us. We could have visitors but no visitors up in our room. May would come visit me all the time. Every chance me and my girls got we would go to May's house just to get away from the shelter setting for the day.

Throughout staying there I met a couple girls my age that had kids as well. However only one female that I still communicate until this day, her name is Saundra. Saundra was so dark skinned but she had the prettiest face ever. She was just a natural black beautiful woman. We had a very good friendship. I am glad that we met.

Time was ticking I only had a couple months left in the shelter and still didn't find a place to live. I filled out applications for a housing authority. I called millions of landlord about apartments for rent. Nothing. I was receiving cash assistance from the county office. They agreed that if I found a place they could pay rent for one year. I was starting to get a little hopeless. Then I called one more landlord and he said that I could come look at the apartment.

My girls and I went to go see the apartment and immediately I accepted it. It was only one bedroom, but the bedroom was huge. The county gave us a furniture voucher so I was able to furnish the apartment. I brought this big bed that had another slide out bed attached to it. I could have used it for my girls however they were still small so they slept with me.

I was so proud of myself. Even though I had assistance with my rent for one year, I still made the effort myself to step out on faith and go to that shelter. I trusted God that he would help me through it and he did.

I did not have a vehicle. We caught the bus just about everywhere we went. I had my stroller so I was good. I was never the person that likes asking anyone to do anything for me. I was never the type to depend on others. So as long as they made buses and I had legs to walk. I did exactly that.

Chapter 14
Love at First Site

Having my own apartment was amazing.
There were two things that I did not like. One, there was
people who were always hanging around in my hallway.
They were actually on drugs and probably drug dealers as
well. This one girl stood out from them though. Her name

was Nia. Nia started speaking to me and we became associates. I think it was really about what I could offer her. Which was not much because I did not have much.

The second thing that bothered me was the Haitian man across the street that kept speaking to me and knocking on my door to give my kids snacks. He did not speak much English at all. Half of the time I did not know what he was saying.

I met a couple of my neighbors. This lady and I hit it off really well. She had kids as well but much older than mine. Me and her played cards a lot, we drank and sometimes smoked. She allowed her son to do these things as well. I was very young at that age and I trusted very easily. That friendship changed me and my kids lives and not in a good way. Be careful who you let in your life and especially who let around your children.

I began to regret moving there. See some things are meant to be learning experiences. It's whether we learn from it or not.

May was still coming over from time to time. One day she actually proposed to me and I had accepted. The ring she gave me was so beautiful. I couldn't believe that we were going to get married.

Nia was telling me that her boyfriend, Lee needed her hair done. She knew I braided hair so I offered to do his hair. When I saw Lee walk into my house it was love at first site. I began combing his hair, he had long gorgeous hair. Hair was my weakness. It was a turn on for me to play in a good grain of hair. When he sat in between my legs, I knew it was a wrap. Only because my body began to have a reaction that it never had for a man.

Lee and I had become really good friends. We talked on the phone all the time. Even at night time we stayed up late on the phone talking until we both fell asleep on the phone. What we had was very special. I drove around with him a lot. When we met he was living with his mom. Lee also told me about a relationship that he had that was on and off with this lady from New Brunswick.

We shared a lot about our lives with each other. I let him know some of my struggles and he told me some of his. I had never had a friend like him that I could ever confide in the way I could with him.

One day May was over my house. There was a knock on the door. I went to the door and it was Lee. He came in and introduced himself to May. He did not stay long at all. I walked him to the door and he left. Once he left May got a little upset. She asked if he and I were messing around, of course I said no and that was the truth. She said that she can see the way Lee and I looked at each that we have feelings for each other. When she said that, it opened my eyes to see that maybe she was right.

May and I decided to call off the engagement and part our ways. We were still friends but we weren't together anymore.

One day I decided to have a little get together at my house. I invited my sister from my dad side. I invited her for a reason. I knew that Lee was a great friend and a great person so I wanted to hook him up with my sister. I felt like she deserved to have a good man.

She came over. We all had some drinks and the music was playing. We all got up and started dancing, having lots of fun. We had our beer in our hands while we were dancing. Both of us were dancing with Lee. My sister on one side and me on the other side. Next thing u know I spilled some of my beer on Lee. I tried to wipe it off, but one thing led to another and next thing you know we were kissing on the dance floor.

I knew my sister was looking at me like I was crazy because here I am trying to hook them to up, and all along I guess I had had feelings for him. That night my life had changed. That moment, that kiss, had led to a new chapter in my life.

Lee and I began seeing each other after that. I gave him a key to my house so that he could come and go as he pleased. Nia had gone away for a month or so, so she had no idea that this was going on. Lee and I became intimate and it was so amazing. He taught me so much about my body as a woman that I never knew. Most of the time we were at his moms house though. It was just more peaceful there.

Lee treated me like a woman. He treated me special. One day Nia came back around hanging in the hallway like usual, and her and Lee got into it because all of her addict friends told her that Lee is at my house all the time. So long story short she asked me and I told her yes, we were seeing each other. Before you know it, they had broken up. I had Lee all to myself. I was quite happy about that.

Chapter 15
New Levels

Things were going great with Lee and I. So great that Nia was very jealous. One day I came home and my back door had been pried open with a crow bar. She had got her friends to break into my mom and steal my stuff so they could get money for they drugs. I knew she had something to do with it because she didn't show up to the hallway that day.

At that point in time I knew that it was not safe to stay there anymore. I began looking for a new home. Right in the midst of me looking for a home, I get a letter from the housing authority saying that I was approved. That was nothing but God. I took all my information to them and right away we moved out East Trenton in a two bedroom apartment. I was so happy, words could not explain. Now I didn't have to worry about people hanging in my hallway.

My girls had they own room and I had my own room. Or should I say Lee and I had our own room. He was there majority of the time so it might as well been his.

A little while afterwards, Lee ends up losing his job. He went downhill from there. He slipped back into old habits and things that hindered his life. He was in and out. I did not see him for days sometimes. I found out that I was pregnant. He went to a couple doctor's appointments. We found out it was a boy. We decided to name him after Lee. I was happy that we were having a boy. My first boy with him but not his first boy. Lee was a little older than me. He had kids my age. It did not matter though.

When it was time for me to have little Lee, Big Lee did not make it to the birth. I was very upset. He showed up hours later. I could not understand what was going on with him. He looked at Lee and cried. He kissed and hugged him all night.

After going home from the hospital everything was back to normal. I was now a mother of three. I enjoyed being a mom. I was so glad that God watched over me as a child. I could have easily been pregnant as a minor. It's no joke. It happens every day in society. I was fortunate enough not be in that category.

Lee and I were still together. He still had his struggles and all. Time was flying. In September of 2008, I find out that I am pregnant again. That was exactly one month before little Lee first birthday. I could not believe this. I told Lee about it. He was never the type to tell me to get an abortion.

Little Lee first birthday party Lee does not show up. I was so hurt. I had no clue what to do.

The drama began to roll in. I would call his phone from time to time and some girl would answer the phone saying that she his girlfriend and that they have been together for years.

That day my heart dropped. I explained to her that he and I had been together for awhile and that we had one son and another baby on the way. She said he denied it, she put him on the phone and his direct word to me was," Nicole this is my girlfriend." I thought my life was over. I could not understand why he would hurt me like this.

I was still in so much denial. How could one man be so busy? When I met him he was in the middle of a divorce, he had Nia as his girlfriend, now me and the girl in New Brunswick. How can you possibly juggle so many women? I was mad at him; I wasn't taking his phone calls so he showed up at the house. He had a key so he let himself in.

He tried to explain himself, but I really did not want to hear it. He explained that he and the girl were having so many issues in the relationship, that they were broken up when he and I met. He just needed time to try and get out of the relationship. I believed him so I stayed with him.

In the mean time I found out that I was having a boy. Having two boys and two girls I put in a transfer for the housing authority for a bigger apartment. Just so happen there was an open spot a couple doors down from my sister Kendal and my biological mom. They told me about it and I asked the housing authority if I could move in it. They approved it. I moved there into a three bedroom. I gave Lee a key to that one to. It was a little easier for me anyway because my biological mom babysit while I took care of business at times.

Lee's habit began to get stronger and stronger. He began to take things from me. I had no clue what to do. The only good thing about that is that he did turn around and give back portions of what he took. I felt so alone. There were times that I called his mom and everyone claimed that they didn't know where he was. Next thing you know he would popup saying that he was getting himself together.

It was time for me to have my son Isaiah. I had him May 2007. Once again Lee missed the birth and showed up hours later. I started putting two and two together. I knew that he was trying to hide this from that girl. It was cool because I knew that all things would come to light.

Chapter 16
Anxiety

After having Isaiah I began working at the daycare center that all four of them were attending. Also that August after having him, I started college. I wanted to be a social worker. Lee was only coming every once in awhile. The drama between this girl and I didn't stop. When Lee was with me she would leave messages on my phone. One message she left is that Lee said I was just a dike on assistance who wanted to have kids by him.

At that point I knew I could not trust him anymore. I knew some of what she said was true because how else would she have known that I was interested in women if he didn't tell her. At that moment I had felt hurt and betrayal. I could not believe this was happening. When I first met Lee I saw things in him that I did not see in other men, but I guess I was wrong. I should have known all men were the same.

It crossed my mind a couple times to go back with women. It was nothing that I was over. It's just that when I was with Lee he made me forget about a woman. There were times that I didn't hear nor see Lee.

After being in school, working and being a fulltime mom, one day it all came down on me.

I was so anxious to go to school the next day because I wanted to find out my score on my math test. The day before my teacher had given me a compliment.

He said that I was his best math student in the class. Others in the class did not catch on as fast as I did.

I had just got off of work. A couple hours later I left to go to school. The school was right downtown so I walked there every class day. I began walking down the street, through the alley to the next street. As I walked, my eyes began to close and every time I opened them and made an attempt to walk, they closed over and over again.

I began to panic. My heart began to race and pound heavily. As I looked up at the street it seemed as if the school was getting further away. In a panic I hurried up and turned around heading back to the house. I made it as far as to my sister's house and sat down in her hallway. They called the ambulance and I got rushed to the hospital.

Once I got there they began asking me what happened. I explained everything to them. They said it sounded like a panic/anxiety attack. They gave me a prescription for some anxiety pills. I did not like taking medicine so I did not get it filled. I was so scared of what happened that I stopped going to school. I stopped walking through the same alley in fear that I would have another anxiety attack.

It seemed like every time I stepped foot out the house, my body would shake, and it felt like I was different. It felt like I was not alive. Like I was here on earth but like I was having an outer body experience.

One day I left the house to go somewhere and I had the worse attack ever. From my feet too my head started to tingle. Everything began to get numb. I was rushed to the hospital. Soon as I got there they injected me with a shot of Ativan. Ativan was a drug for anxiety. Soon as they injected it the tingling went away.

Once again they asked me what happened. I explained what happened. They began asking me deeper questions about my past. I told them everything starting from a child and up. At that moment they had diagnosed me with PTSD. Post Traumatic Stress Disorder. They prescribed me with more medication, and suggested that I sought counseling. Counseling was the last thing on my mind. I was not about to go and talk to someone that I did not even know about my problem.

At this point I could not believe that this was happening to me. But then again I always felt like the odd child so why not me.

When I got home this time, I lay in my bed and cried. I hugged my children so tight. I felt so lost. More lost than I ever did even as a child. I had no one to turn to.

I felt so embarrassed about it so I could not talk to my family. Lee was not around so I could not even talk to him. Still until this day I don't even think he knows that this happened to me.

After the third anxiety attack, I gave up. I would not go out the house anymore. I stayed inside the house. I stopped going to work, I had already stopped going to school. I stopped living altogether. I literally stayed in the house for 6 months straight. I stopped eating. My mom and sister had to go grocery shopping for me. They did everything for me that had to be done outside the house.

After awhile my body could not eat anything heavy. For breakfast I ate cereal, for lunch I ate cereal, and for dinner I ate cereal. I lost about forty pounds over the course of those six months. I still fed my kids and took care of them. But anything that consists on going outside the house I did not do.

Chapter 17
Back In the Game

After those long six months, I was getting a little weary. I got tired of letting the devil rule over my life and keep me bound. One day I got up and went to church. Afterwards I felt so rejuvenated. However through the whole service I was jittery, paranoid, you name it, and I was it. I could not sit still. I thought people were staring at me.

I had enough strength to get out and buy me a car. That was a start. My first car was a Honda accord. It was small but we all packed up in there. It got us from A to Z. I did not have to worry about asking no one for a ride or walking or catching the bus. I could leave on my own time and return on my own time.

I did not decide to go back to college however I did decide to go to medical school. I wanted to major as a Medical Assistant. I invited my oldest brother girlfriend (rest in peace Duke. My oldest brother is no longer here with us) to come to school with me. Her name was Sammy. Sammy was funny as hell. She kept me laughing throughout the entire school day.

While I was in school, Lee began to come back around. I loved that because I missed him, but I hated the situation. I just tried to keep my focus on school, Lord knows I did not want to get really stressed out and have a bad anxiety attack again. I was already still on edge.

One day Lee came to the house. He brought his half brother Jake with him. They shared the same father that's what made them half brothers. They didn't look just alike but they both had similar features. He brought him over a couple times to the house but not much.

As time went on I ended up graduating from medical school in September 2009. I had my graduation and soon after, I started my externship. Right after my externship hours the doctor's office hired me. I was so happy that I did such a good job, that they decided to keep me.

That November I wanted to do something for my birthday. Lee, Jake, my sister Kendal, and her best friend Char decided to go out to the club. We were having so much fun, dancing around and drinking. I always talked to lee about us getting married. His response was always, in due time. Whatever that meant.

I was so excited to see my present from him. I just knew it was an engagement ring. I guess my feelings were hurt. Soon as Lee looked at my facial expression, he knew I was disappointed. He said to me, I know that you didn't get what you wanted but in due time. Those were his favorite words.

That night we went back home. We did grown up things and called it a night. He couldn't stay because he had his brother with him. So I said goodnight and he left.

About a month later I found out that I had another sister on my biological dad side. Her name was Latonya. When I first met her, I knew that she was in relation. I saw all the similar features. I immediately felt like she was always a part of me because we clicked instantly. She has a great and funny personality. I wish we could have met earlier in life. Now we have a lot of catching up to do.

Anyhow, I found out that he was back in bad habits. It was not as bad this time because he still had his truck and all. He was still coming to see me. Still had a key to my house so he could still come and go as he pleases.

One day while I was at work. I called Lee phone on my break. Guessed who answered, not him the girl from New Brunswick. So we get into it, next thing you know she say, that's my husband, we got married last year. I said oh yea well tell your husband to bring me my house keys and its over between me and him.

Apparently she must have delivered the message because he didn't call me back, he showed up at the house that night. I asked for my keys and for an explanation. He wouldn't give me an explanation. Instead he tried to leave. So I told him he not going nowhere until he explained to me why did he lead me on knowing that he was planning a whole life with another woman.

He jumped in his truck, so I jumped on top of the front hood of his truck. He drives off around the corner, than pulls over to try to get me off the roof of his truck. I got down and grabbed this metal pole. I than got back on top and swung at his windshield. The whole windshield shattered. He got out the truck and smacked me so hard in my face that I fell to the ground. He hit me so hard that my wig fell off. Then he got in the truck and sped off.

Once I got my wig back on, I ran around the corner and jumped into my car to chase him. He was long gone; however I knew exactly where he was headed. Or should I say I guessed. I headed straight to his mom house. Soon as I pulled up he was getting out the truck. He came over to me and said, no Nicole, not here, not at my mom's house. He said lets go somewhere and talk.

We both hoped in our vehicles and pulled off. He sped off again. So I'm chasing him all over the town. On and off of highways and everything. Finally he went down this curvy dark road and I lost him. I was pissed, I cried for days. My first broken heart. I never expected that Lee would have been the one to break my heart. Or was all the signs there but I failed to see them?

How could I have known he had planned another marriage when I didn't even know he got the divorce from the first wife that he was separated from. Oh yeah boy was I a fool. After that day I told myself that I never wanted another man.

Chapter 18
Trapped

After things had died down, Lee eventually came back around because we had kids together. He had to see his kids. It was hard to let go of something that you thought would last. Even though I found out the truth, I still was intimate with him. I guess a part of me did not want to let him go.

A lot started to change. He began to not answer the phone as much; he would hide his phone in his truck at night when he was home with his wife. It was just too much to handle for me. I began to feel like I was playing myself and I began to realize that no matter how much I was intimate with him, he still did not belong to me and that he was not going to be coming home to me at night anymore.

I began to make myself available again. Why should I sit at home crying when he wasn't crying over me while he was going back and forth between me and her? Nope not anymore.

Lee had decided to go away to Florida for awhile. Of course I was going to miss him but another part of me was like, he not my man and I refuse to be anyone side piece anymore. We were intimate that one last time before he left.

Days later his brother Jake showed up. He gave me the biggest hug ever. He had informed me that Lee told him to keep coming to check on us while he was away. The more he came the more he hugged me when he got there and before he left. The hugs started to last longer and longer.

I was not thinking at the time that this is Lee brother. All I knew is that when he hugged me, I felt something. One day we sat down on the couch. We both recognized that we felt a certain way about each other. We started drinking and next thing you know we were intimate that one time. We stopped in the middle of the act.

Both of us felt bad about it afterwards. All I did was tell Jake how he reminded me so much of Lee. They have the same eyes, and all. Every time I looked at Jake I thought about Lee. I knew they were two different people but all I saw was the similarity in Jake that I saw in Lee. Lee is who I wanted but I could not have him. Jake just came around at the wrong time and I was vulnerable. Part of me thinks that Jake did this on purpose. Lee told me years later that Jake use to always say he want a ride a die girl like me. Had I would have known all of this than I would have never took the bait and fell into Jakes trap.

I found out I was pregnant. I immediately told Lee being that Lee and I were intimately before he left. I had no intentions on telling Jake because there was no way it was his baby. When Lee got back in town, he rubbed my belly a lot. I was not too thrilled about being pregnant because I am smart enough to know a baby don't keep a man, if anything it would have made the situation worse.

One day I went to church and we had a visitor there. Her name was Tina. I introduced myself to her. She and I hit it off right away. She had never had a relationship with a women but she was very friendly and giggly and such a sweet girl. She was older than me by a couple of years. She was not from the area so everything was new to her. She had a boyfriend that was way older than her.

Tina and I found out that our birthdays were a couple days apart. We both were Scorpios. We began seeing each other. This was her first relationship with a woman, but of course not mines. This was all I needed to take my mind off of men. I was never going to let another man break my heart the way that Lee did.

I put in for a transfer to a bigger unit. I ended up having my son Jayden in 2010. Two days later they called me to move. I had just got out of the hospital. No one was around to help me move so I had to pay two men who were on my street to help me move everything in my van. Every time I needed someone they were never there for me.

Once I got settled in I was so happy. I had a four bedroom apartment and it was huge. As Jayden began to get older by the day, I started noticing that his face and body was changing. Changes to similarities of Jake. So I sent Jake some pictures to see if he felt the same. He said that it was impossible because we did not go through with the act. I don't know if he was in denial or what, but he started posting pictures of him and the baby on social media. People started commenting saying they looked just alike. At this point I was puzzled.

I had a get together at my house. Lee showed up. Tina was there too. A lot of family came over. I had food and drinks. Non alcoholic of course. Lee and I went into the back room alone. He looks at the baby and he says Jake is on social media saying that the baby is his. At that moment I had to face the truth. Lee knew that Jake and I had slept together. He was hurt and angry at me for a very long time.

Until this day he believes that I did this to get back at him. I did not do this intentionally. I did not ask Jake to come check on us. Lee did. I take full responsibility for the part I did play. Did I feel bad for what I did? Yes none of us ever got a paternity test, since Jayden looked like Jake; I just assumed that he was Jakes. I knew that Lee was relieved that he didn't have to go back and explained to his wife that I was having his baby again. That still does not exclude the fact that he was sleeping with me.

Chapter 19
Commitment

As time went on, I had so much on my mind. Tina and I had become best friends. We did a lot together. Hung out a lot together. Lee and I did not talk too much. He still came every once in a blue moon to get his kids. Not as often as he should. What did I expect he had his own life with his own step kids that he treated better than his own kids.

Jake was around more often now. I found out that he was trying to end his relationship with another woman in New Brunswick. Come to find out the girl was Lee's wife sister. When I found out this I wanted to die. Wow so both brothers are involved with sisters. If this equation can get any worse. Jake was mad at me because he wanted to be with me as his girlfriend. I did not want to do that because of his brother.

We would argue a lot about it. Just because I felt bad about how I was doing Lee, Jake would throw in my face that he thinks I still loved Lee. Jake use to say Lee out living his life happy so why couldn't we be happy. I never said lets be together but actions speak louder than words, next thing you know Jake was at my house all the time.

Than I had to deal with the drama from the girl he was dealing with. Come to find out the car he was driving was hers. I would look in his phone and see that she was cursing him out cause he takes her car and be gone all the time. Of course he denied it though even with proof. It mattered but then again, he and I were not a couple anyway.

I started going to my home church more often. The more I went the more I wanted to change some things in my life. I knew that things were not right. I told Jake that I could not be with him. I told him that I wanted to do the right thing. He said he understood. So I'm guessing he ran back to New Brunswick to the sister house. Actually truth be told he had never left there. He was always with her.

I was going to church faithfully. I had began ministry on the choir and singing on the praise team. I liked doing that. It made me feel good and closer to God. I actually felt like I was doing something good for once.

At church I had met a couple of friends. Of course you know Tina is one. And some girl named Nina. Nina was a good friend too. I learned to build relationships with people before I call them my friends. Nina cousin came to the church. His name was Ron. When I looked at him, I knew he looked familiar. This was Sherry's ex husband. If you all don't remember who Sherry is, she is the lady I met at the college program when I was fifteen. Her mom is the one who let me stay with them for one year.

Anyhow, Ron joined the choir too. One day after church he was talking about he made good lasagna. So he offered to cook for me. I saw no problem with it. So we began talking. He said that he was interested in me, so we decided to date. Two weeks into being with him. He asked me to marry him. I said yes because I thought I was doing the right thing by God. I did not love him nor was I in love with him. It all was moving too fast. During that time, we were intimate one time. I ended up getting pregnant with my daughter Mia.

I was so disgusted that I broke up with Ron. People at church convinced me to get back with him. I kept telling them I did not love him. I got back with him about 3 times, than the very last time I called it quits for good. I just could not go through with it; all I could see was me marrying someone I had no feelings for.

It all happened so fast that we never got a chance to get to know each other. A little while after that I got back with Jake. Once Ron found out than all of a sudden the baby was not his. His family was going around saying it was Jakes baby. I said to myself I'm glad they was there in the bed with me with I was with either or, since they swear they know what's going on.

Jake was there throughout my whole pregnancy. Once I had Mia in 2012 and everyone saw her picture than all of a sudden it was Ron's baby. I should have still made him take a test just to be smart. It didn't matter if it was his baby anyway because Jake raised her, and she called Jake dad. Ron came around to see her once in a blue moon. And I do mean a blue moon. He gave me money for her whenever he had a job. It was never consistent though. He changed jobs like I changed my underwear. I was on and off of assistance. Every time I reapplied they made me sign up for child support, I had no choice but too or I could not get cash assistance.

One thing I hated is that I always started things and never finished it. Every time I got a job, I did not keep it no more than three months. It was rather sad. I always made sure I kept a roof over my kids head. They were my everything. They were the reason why I lived. I could have still been out there living a crazy life, however once I had my first born, I chose to grow up.

Chapter 20
Lies, lies, lies

Once Jake and I were with each other. We began having issues. I got sick of feeling like I was always the other women. He was still driving the girl's car and they were still going back and forth arguing. He always made it seem like it was her. In order to find the truth I had to look into his phone. He was an alcoholic so he was always being caught off guard.

Every time I wanted to know something I found the truth out in his phone. I was so mad because it felt like I was doing a repeat of what I went through with Lee. I had a birthday that had just passed. He gave me this watch that had a pink plastic band and rhinestones around the rim. I should have known something was up with it because it did not come in a box. Nothing he gave me came in a box.

One day I was going through his phone and I read a message from the girl. She was asking did he see her watch and her bracelet, and if he had it she wanted it back. So I responded, letting her know it was me. I said what does the watch look like because he had just given me a watch for my birthday. She described the watch to a complete detail. I said I have your watch and don't worry I will be sending it back with him.

Of course with proof he denied it. He always denied everything. I saw all the red flags but continued to ignore them. Somewhere in the mix I had our son Joe'l in 2015. Sometimes we had good moments; however the bad outweighed the good. Every time we got into an argument he always brought up Lee. He said that I treat Lee better than him when Lee was not in his kid's life like Jake was. So he always said he thinks I still loved Lee. I never told him that but he was right.

See I was forced to stop loving Lee because my heart was broke when I found out Lee was married. So I put my feelings for him on the back burner.

Jake felt like every since I had my daughter Mia that I changed and I got mean, but he don't realize that the things he put me through made me that way. The lies he constantly told me. He never helped me out with bills nor gave me money, well correction if he did give me money it was about five dollars. He was in his kid's life however he did not provide for them.

Every time we got into an argument, sometimes I would hit him, other times I would put him out and he would run back to sleep at the girl house in New Brunswick. I see she was really stupid like I was. I was in fear of being alone and starting over.

There were times I tried to get him to go to church with me but he only went on holidays. All the attention that I sought from him, he sought from me so there was no way I could sit back and be the woman in the relationship. Yet he got mad when I acted like the boss. He was so depressed all he wanted to do was drink.

I was getting a little weary. I cried. Sometimes I even talked to Lee on the phone. He always knew when something was wrong with me. He kept warning me and telling me how much of a snake he was but of course I did not listen.

One year later I got pregnant with my last daughter Jayla. That made the eighth child to my tribe. Before I had her. So much was going on. Jake was stealing from me. He was going out on the corners talking to his friends and chilling outside with my neighbors for about six hours straight every day.

Yes he walked the big kids to school; yes he picked the big kids up from school, However that was not enough. Sometimes when I had temp jobs he would watch them, but I could not work in peace. I got a phone call every darn minute complaining about something the kids did. Even when he got mad at me he would walk off and leave so than I couldn't go to work.

It was just getting to the point where I had to hide my pocket book. One day I locked it in my car. He found my spare key and still went in the and stole my money. He never had remorse for anything he did. He never apologized either. Yes I was guilty of having an attitude and exploding when he did something to me.

When I was pregnant with Jayla he got so mad at me and tried to choke me and threw me up against the door. I never called anyone into my problems. I always handled my own. I had wanted to leave him for a long time now but never had the strength to.

Since I was pregnant I had to sit down from singing on the worship team and dance ministry. I completely understood. I was not happy but I did understand. How could I be ministering to others when I am not right myself? I loved God, there was not questioning about that. I was still learning a lot.

Chapter 21
Decisions

After I had my daughter Jayla in 2016, Jake came to the hospital. I was already having car issues so he did make it there. He stayed at the hospital for a little while, but then he left to take the kids to my biological mom house. She was going to watch them while I was in the hospital. He said he would be back later on.

He never showed up. He stopped answering the phone. I could not reach him. So I called my neighbor to go knock on the door. She tells me that he is across the street chilling at my other neighbor's house which was a female. She also had a brother that lived there. So my neighbor gives him the phone, we start arguing and he hangs up on me. I did not hear from him until the next day. I was pissed because I could not leave the hospital. I had no control over what happened that night. No matter what he says in my heart I believe that he slept with her that night. No one can convince me otherwise.

Once I got home from the hospital, nothing was done. The same day I came home cleaning up. Another reason to piss me off. I just don't understand men. If you know I'm going to fuss about things than stop doing those things. How hard is it?

One night Jake got mad at me and told me that no man will ever want me for more than having a baby and just sex. People say words don't hurt. That night words hurt me. I picked up that nail polish remover with acetone and threw it in his eyes. He cried like a big baby so I had to hurry up and flush his eyes out so I didn't have to go to jail that night.

The last straw that took the icing on the cake is the night he went across the street drinking. Once again I was in the house tending to my responsibilities. I just so happened to look out the window, I saw him and some young girls running around and one of the girls run up to him and grabs his butt. I ran outside and confronted them, but once again I was in the wrong. At least that's what he made it seem like.

That night I was just so upset with the lies, disrespect, the flirting in my face everywhere we go, the stealing from me. You name it, he did it. I was tired, I threw all is crap out the window and told him I was done. I had reached my limits……….

We were officially over. He still came to see his kids. He still got them on the weekends. He told my oldest son to lie and say that he was catching the train to get them, when he really was using the girl car in New Brunswick. The reason I knew is that every time my son Jayden saw this type of car, he would say there go dada train. He had confused the hell out of my son. He was young; he did not know any better.

It's just a shame how manipulating one human being can be. They tell so many lies that they can't even keep up with them.

I started drinking more and smoking cigarettes again. I started hanging out with a couple of my neighbors because it seemed like we all had broke up with our men around the same time. Just about every day I got drunk and cried because of hurt and pain I felt. I couldn't lie I was lonely, but I did not miss what he put me through.

I started associating with my neighbor's brother across the street. People started going back telling him that I was hanging with him. So what, I was free to hang with whomever I wanted. So now until this day he has accused me of being intimate with him. He says it was his friend. However it was my neighbor that he talked to once in a blue moon. He did not know this man from a can of paint.

I find it rather hilarious how a man can brush off what they have done to hurt you, but soon as they feel like you have done something to them, they announce it to the world like they so hurt. Please……………………… After a couple weeks I started to feel a little better.

I was having issues with my landlord. They were not fixing anything, my carpet needed to be changed and I needed a paint job. I called the city on them because I noticed wholes in my walls that had mold. I notified the landlord and still nothing. Once the city got involved. They immediately fixed all the problems. They get mad every time someone calls the city on them, but I had no choice. I did not want my kid's asthma getting messed up again. I called them because my daughter Kaiasia woke up one day and could not breathe. I tried to grab the asthma machine, but her face started turning blue. I called 911. It seemed like they was taking forever to get there.

They got there, put her on oxygen. They took her to a local hospital, when we got there, she was defecating on herself. I thought my baby girl was gone. They put a breathing tube down her throat and transferred us to The Children's Hospital in Philadelphia. She stayed on the tube for about a week. They slowly weaned her off and she began breathing on her own. I was so grateful that God had pulled her through that.

Like I said though that is the reason why I called the city. I actually call them while I was sitting in the hospital watching my daughter on a machine.

Chapter 22
Back to square one

My landlord was not happy that I called the city. When we got out the hospital, I had so much to do. My landlord kept showing up at my home unannounced taking pictures of my home on the spot. They showed up three times. When I told them I was not letting them in because they are supposed to give me 24 hour notice they threatened to bring the cops. So I opened the door each time.

They took me to court saying that I did not pass any of their house visits. They said the house was not clean in certain areas. Well what do you expect when you are breaking the law showing up purposely soon as I get out of bed with your camera? They wanted revenge. I went to court and they said either I can sign a voluntary removal letter or they can have another court date and have me evicted. The last thing I wanted to do was get evicted. So I just left on my own.

My sister Kendal said we could come stay with her. No one was around like usual to help me move, so I took whatever I could in my van. Brand new beds for my children, I had to leave. I had to start off fresh again. I found a job at a restaurant while I was staying there. Jake started coming over; we had decided to work things out. I was cool with it until I went in his phone and found out he was talking to some lady. I got mad at him and I told him, it was over again.

See what he did not understand is that whatever happens when we are broken up is different, however when we get back together it should be just him and I. But each time we got back together he always brings baggage back into the relationship. He says to me that I had a friend too. Yes I did but when he and I got back together there was never any drama from a third party, only when it came to his flings.

I ended up getting let go from my job. Apparently they felt like I did not fit in well with their company. No problem. I found another job at the college in Princeton. It was a temp job. Once I found a job I found a three bedroom apartment. It wasn't the best, but at least we had a roof over our heads. I hated the area I was in. I prayed everyday that we would be blessed with a better situation. I felt down a lot. Did not really feel like I had anyone to talk to. Tina and I was not friend anymore. She had left her relationship and moved out of town with some stranger she met online. One day we went to go visit her. She showed off and talked about my kids. So I dismissed her as my friend. Never spoken with her since and I would not change that. I am good with my decision.

I still talked to Nina every once in awhile. I still kept my guard up with her as well because she has a situation that was similar to mine, where she has secrets. See the difference is that people know that I have been in crazy situations so I don't hide anything. So if she was capable of that than who knows what else she capable of. Those I don't trust won't be in my circle.

We moved in. the kids were excited. If they was happy than so was I. Financially I still struggled. I filed my taxes and they were taken for student loans. I had nothing. I had no one. Thank God I am out of default today as we speak.

Jake always seems to show up. Never there when its help needed though with moving. The way that u can tell who he is dating is to look at his car. It was never his, always the woman's car. He was the same person, nothing had changed. It's crazy because I left him to see if anything would change and what does he do each time? He runs to the next woman.

This time he ran to the opposite race. He knew that she would be even more stupid than I was. She was another reason for us to argue because like I said he would never be truthful. I would have to go through his phone like usual. I guess I felt like since him and I was still intimate that I still had some control over what he did. Neither did I realize that he did what he wanted anyway.

It got to the point when I would drive up there to his dad house, which is where he lived. Every day I got mad at him, I drove up there. He would tell me he out of town and I drive there and he getting out the car with the girl. I have confronted them on numerous occasions. All he would do is act funny in my face like he wasn't just at my house. I started showing her pictures of him in my bed and messages he sent me. She did not care. She was married. Yes he told me everything. His little sister got mad at him one day and for a whole week she told me him and the girls every move. That's how I knew when and what time to show up.

It all got so overwhelming for me. He told me that every time he stop talking with these women to get back with me that I end up kicking him out again. I got tired of making myself look like a fool, so I said forget it. I went about my business. I stayed to myself. I did not want any more men. I tried a couple of dating sites but they all seemed like a bunch of horny dogs so I deleted those apps.

At this point I just put all my focus on my babies. What mattered the most is that they needed me to be in my right mind so that I can be the mom that God had appointed me. I knew I was not perfect; however I was a working progress.

Chapter 23
New Beginnings

My job out Princeton ended. I did not know what to do or how I was going to pay my rent. I went to the temp service to sign up to work at the warehouse. I hated that labor work. Standing up packing boxes for eight hours. While I was there I was online on social media. I came across someone who was advertising jobs. It was located in Philadelphia. I applied for the job and they scheduled me for the interview.

The day of the interview I drove to Philadelphia. The job site was only about twenty minutes from where I lived in Jersey. Long story short, I got the job. I went through all the pre hire steps and right afterwards I started work. I was traveling back in forth for training. Training was actually one hour away from Jersey. I had to go to training for seven days.

By the fourth days I began to get weary. I almost gave up. I didn't have the gas money that I needed to keep commuting to that one drive. I thought about my kids and how they were depending on me, so I pushed through the rest of the week.

The next day after training I started work at my job site. That was March 2017. I was so excited that I was actually doing something that I loved doing. Which is taking care of others. I work in homes with adults who have disabilities.

A little while after getting the job. I was on social media and I ran across one of Rosaline posts. She posted a house for rent in Philadelphia. I messaged her and asked if I could fill out an application. There were a couple other candidates on the list as well. The kids and I drove up to see the house. We fell in love with it immediately. About a couple days later Rosaline said that we were approved to move into the house. We were so excited.

I knew that was no one but God. I was not even thinking about moving up to Philadelphia. It never crossed my mind but all along it was in God's plan for me. We moved in our new home April of 2017. We were so blessed. Words could not even express how grateful we were.

We were all settled into the home. The kids had made it into the last semester of school. The girls did not like they school, neither did I, however we did not have a choice at that time. I loved the elementary school. Very good school.

I worked seven days a week with no days off. This was my permanent schedule. It was a little crazy because I could not be home with my kids like I wanted to in the evening. I ran into a couple obstacles with neighbors who did not know us. But it was no obstacle that God could not bring us through.

Jake came over like twice before. Other than those two times there was really no need for him to come. I tried to establish boundaries with him, however when I was at work, he would make excuses for why he had to come inside whenever he picked and dropped the kids off. He would not respect my boundaries. All I knew is that I did not want him in my life and it was going to stay that way.

The first year was very tricky with rent and bills. I almost was let it get the best of me, however I got a hold of it and I made things work. My job was not paying so much so I filled out an application for another job that paid more. I got the job so I put in my two weeks' notice. I started training at the other job. Once training was over they told us they did not have work for us right away.

I said to myself this is not going to work because I have to pay rent and other bills. That being said I went back to my old job supervisor; she helped me get my job back. They said that I was a good worker and that's why the reconsidered my recognition. I was so grateful for the decision they had made.

Weeks later I got an email saying that we have to go down and vote for a contract that would pay us two dollars more. The contract got approved and I was making two dollars more. I was so shocked that this was happening. This is why I should have waited to hear from God before I put my two weeks' notice in. All that time he was already in route with a plan before I even decided to leave the company. Once again God is good. I still struggle from day to day but we make it through each day.

The only thing that started to be on my mind after being at work for a couple of months, is that I needed more time with my kids. When I go to work I take my residents out on activities. A lot of those activities I knew my kids would love. I was getting a little depressed because the thing I was doing with my residents is the thing I wanted to do with my kids.

I did not have much vacation and sick time because it didn't kick in with that many hours. Once they started to accumulate a little bit, I could only use it for my children when they were sick and I had to stay home with them. I needed a change.

Chapter 24
Anything is possible

After being at work for a year to be exact, an overnight position came available. The position was overnight for two days only. I did not know who would watch my kids at night; however I stepped out on faith and applied for the position.

Meanwhile I found out that Jake and Lee's dad was in the hospital having heart problems. Like usual, I went up to the hospital. I got into it with Jake because he was up there with a new one; I had to take a good look at her because she looked like a short butch man. I confronted him and of course he lied and said it was his co worker. I than confronted her and she said the same thing.

Their whole demeanor it did not take a rocket science to tell that they had something going on. I did not care anyway because he was not my man. I just hate liars. The real reason why I was there was for his dad anyway. Lee showed up at the hospital later on. After everyone left, Lee and I stayed for a couple more hours. Lee ended up staying the night at his uncle house so he did not have to drive all those hours back home.

The next day we met up at the hospital again. It actually felt good that I could be there to support Lee through his time of need.

About a week later Lee called and said that he was moving in with his uncle in Jersey because him and his wife was separating and getting a divorce. I gave him the option to come stay with me. He was my son's father and no matter what we went through, I would always be there for him. He said that my offer was generous but he was going to stay in Jersey with his Uncle.

During the process I got accepted for the overnight position. So being that Lee lived in Jersey now, he was much closer to me. I asked him could he come over with the kids on the two days that I did overnights for the first week and I would find someone for the second week. He agreed to watch them.

Each night he traveled from jersey to my house to watch the kids. Next thing you know a little bit of drama came about at his uncle house. Things were getting stressful for him there so once again I invited him to my house. He came to stay with me.

We sat down and talked about a lot, he told me he had a lot going on and that he needed to get rid of his baggage. I understood exactly what he was going through.

I never thought for a million years that I would ever have him back in my life. The first month was stressful because I have kids by Jake and that is a lot on Lee to handle. I don't blame him. However he has always treated Jakes kids the same. He cares for them as he does for his own kids.

I don't ever expect for him to ever be comfortable with it all. As we are working things out, it is not easy on both parts. I think that he is cheating every time he walks out the door. And this is not just assuming. I feel like he resents me because sometimes he gets mad and curses at me. He never did that to me in the past. I always question him about things, he hates that. Sometimes I run my mouth just to sabotage the relationship so that he can leave. I have given him the opportunity to walk out the door plenty off times.

Now I drop and pick my kids up from Jakes house. I had to do this because every time Jake picked them up and he saw Lee truck, he always had something negative to say. To avoid less drama I had to provide a way that Jake could not come near my home. I did this because each day I want to prove to Lee that I am sorry for hurting him the way I did.

A lot of days go by, some good some bad. Lee said to me that I am not the person I used to be and that Jake has damaged me. You know what he is actually right. Even though Lee got married while we were together and it broke my heart. Jake has scorned me and damaged me to the point where Lee might give up on me one day and walk out of my life. I know I'm not the only one who has issues. Lee does to. Sometimes I feel like he nitpicks with me than when it turns into an argument, than I'm the one wrong because I don't stop running my mouth. Every time we argue we both say things that we regret.

On August 14, 2018, we get into an argument early in the morning. You could tell that he was already not in a good mood. I just hate when people always point out the bad things in you, instead of seeing your good qualities. But yet those same people always point the finger at others instead of themselves.

Lee is also a child of God. He has built a relationship with the Pastor our neighborhood church. Every day is a learning process. Every day that God allows us to see, it's a day to glorify Him.

The best feeling ever is the bond that Lee has developed with our sons. They never had that opportunity before. I am not perfect. Lee is not perfect. I need to first heal from old damaged, if it's even possible.

Who knows what will happen. Lee is a great man. One of the best men that ever came into my life. He has always had my best interest at heart. He has always showed me that he cared about me. I just feel like we have so much anger toward each other and we can't seem to look past it.

(Closing Remarks)

The truth is I am extremely tired and overwhelmed. I can really honestly say that I hate men. I always have and probably always will. It's just a shame to feel so trapped and can't do anything about it. I know I was not born to like women but I know for sure that I was not made to cope with a man. It hurts my heart so deeply to feel this way. However, I know that God is my guidance.

Only God knows what is in store for our lives. Sometimes I say I'm unlovable because I feel like I was damaged since I was five years old and throughout my whole life. Will that feeling ever change I don't know. Will I ever let go and let any man love me and stop putting up a shield. I don't know.

I am going through some struggles, still financially but like I said, God brings us through. I am experiencing some new things with my oldest daughters that let me know that they won't be kids forever, but I still love them all dearly. I am here to guide them. To steer their paths in the right direction. I don't want them to have a generational curse. They do not have to grow up like I did.

I hope that one day my children can read my book and not make the same mistakes as I did. I want others to read my book, and then maybe they can better understand me. Most of all I want the world to read my book as awareness. I hope to change lives and open eyes to reality. And just maybe, just maybe one day my life can be a reflection of hope for someone else's…………………..

Made in the USA
Middletown, DE
31 July 2021